SPORTS

BASEBALL

by Mari Schuh

AMICUS | AMICUS INK

helmet

mound

Look for these words and pictures as you read.

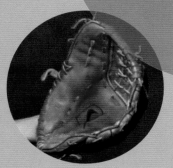

glove

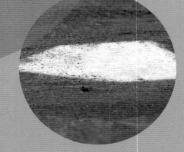

home plate

The pitcher throws the ball.
A baseball game starts.
Play ball!

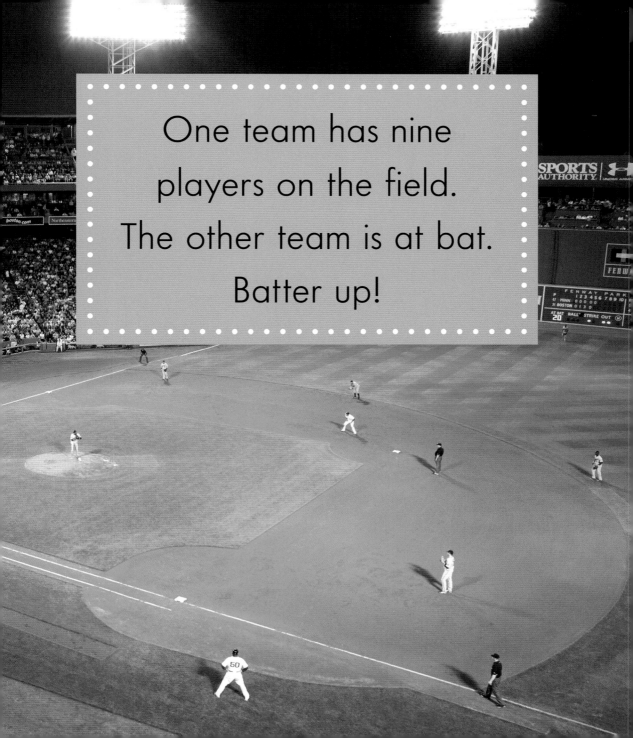

One team has nine
players on the field.
The other team is at bat.
Batter up!

Do you see the helmet?

It is hard.

It keeps the batter safe.

helmet

Do you see the mound?
The pitcher stands there.

mound

glove

Do you see his glove?
He catches the ball.
The batter is out.

Do you see home plate?
A player slides across it.
He scores a run.

home plate

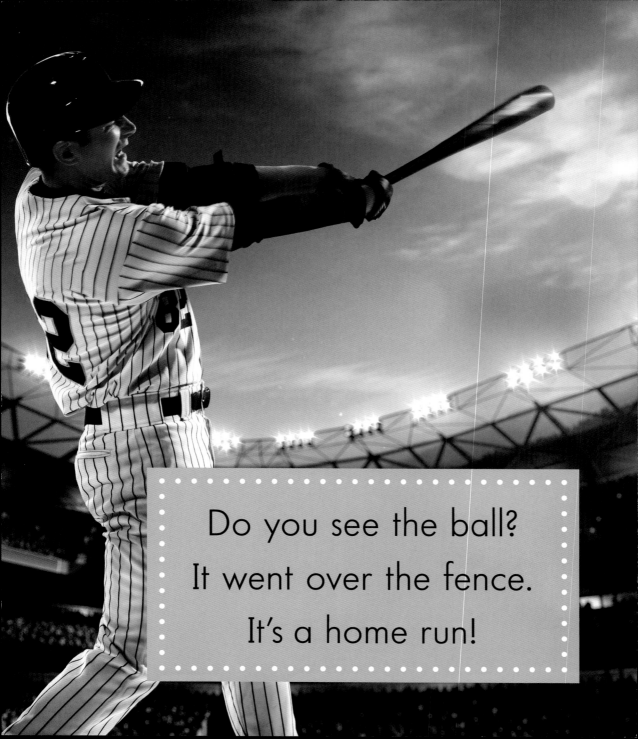

Do you see the ball?
It went over the fence.
It's a home run!

Do you see the helmet?
It is hard.
It keeps the batter safe.

helmet

Do you see the mound?
The pitcher stands there.

mound

helmet

mound

Did you find?

glove

home plate

glove

Do you see his glove?
He catches the ball.
The batter is out.

Do you see home plate?
A player slides across it.
He scores a run.

home plate

Spot is published by Amicus and Amicus Ink
P.O. Box 1329, Mankato, MN 56002
www.amicuspublishing.us

Library of Congress Cataloging-in-Publication Data
Names: Schuh, Mari C., 1975- author.
Title: Baseball / by Mari Schuh.
Description: Mankato, Minnesota : Amicus, [2018] | Series:
  Spot. Sports
Identifiers: LCCN 2016044426 (print) | LCCN 2016051594
  (ebook) | ISBN 9781681510859 (Library Binding) | ISBN
  9781681522043 (pbk.) | ISBN 9781681511757 (E-book) |
  ISBN 9781681511757 (pdf)
Subjects: LCSH: Baseball--Juvenile literature.
Classification: LCC GV867.5 .S35 2018 (print) | LCC
  GV867.5 (ebook) | DDC 796.357--dc23
LC record available at https://lccn.loc.gov/2016044426

Printed in China

HC 10 9 8 7 6 5 4 3 2 1
PB 10 9 8 7 6 5 4 3 2 1

In memory of my brother John —M.S.

Rebecca Glaser, editor
Deb Miner, series and book designer
Ciara Beitlich, production
Holly Young, production

Photos by: Associated Press/Al
Behrman, 1, Jae C. Hong 8-9; Getty
6-7, 12-13; iStock, cover, 2br, 15br;
Shutterstock 3, 4-5, 10-11, 14-15

BASEBALL